JUNIOR BIOGRAPHIES

DONALD TRUMP

BUSINESSMAN AND PRESIDENT

Rita Santos

Enslow Publishing

101 W. 23rd Street
Suite 240
New York, NY 10011
USA

enslow.com

WORDS TO KNOW

contestant A person who takes part in a contest.

discipline The control that helps a person to follow a set of rules.

discriminate To treat a person or group unfairly.

economics The study of how things are made, bought, and sold.

Electoral College People from each state who choose the next president based on who the people in each state vote for.

immigrant A person who comes from another country.

real estate The buying and selling of buildings.

reality television A TV show that doesn't have a script and is meant to show "real life."

secretary of state The person in the government who works with leaders of other countries.

CONTENTS

Donald Trump

CHAPTER 1
GROWING UP

It was 1963. A military student named Donald Trump was marching in the Columbus Day parade in New York City. He looked up at the tall buildings all around him. He wanted to do great things in **real estate** just like his father. But he also had dreams of becoming a famous actor. No matter what goal Donald had, one thing was always the same: Everything had to be big.

THE TRUMP FAMILY

Donald John Trump was born on June 14, 1946, in Queens, which is a part of

Growing up, Donald was good at many sports, especially football, baseball, and soccer.

New York City. His father, Fred, worked in real estate. He was very successful. He mostly built apartment buildings in New York. His mother, Mary, was a Scottish **immigrant** who came to America with little money. Fred and Mary were married in 1936 and had five children. Donald is the second of three sons and has two older sisters.

Donald grew up in this house in Queens, New York.

Donald Says:
"As an adolescent, I was mostly interested in creating mischief."

ACTING OUT

As a child, Donald had lots of energy. He often got in trouble in school for talking when he should have been listening. Some classmates have stated their opinion that he was mean to other students. He hated to lose at games.

In middle school Donald would sneak away from his parents and ride the train into Manhattan on weekends. He explored Central Park with his friends. His father was very strict. He thought Donald's behavior needed to change.

Donald liked to visit Central Park (*right*) in New York City when he was young.

CHAPTER 2
MILITARY SCHOOL

When Donald was thirteen, his father sent him to New York Military Academy to teach him **discipline**. In military school, Donald wore a uniform. He learned to march and follow orders. He became a captain when he was seventeen, which put him in charge of other students.

Donald Trump's nickname is "the Donald."

Donald is seen here wearing his uniform in his 1964 yearbook picture from military school.

As an adult, Donald found that his time in military school was good for him. But as a teenager, he knew the military life was not for him. Donald told his friends that it was his dream to go to film school. But he also wanted to follow in his father's footsteps.

Donald Says:
"You have to think anyway, so why not think big?"

COLLEGE DAYS

After he graduated from military school, Donald went to Fordham University in New York. Even though he already

Donald learned a lot about business when he went to the Wharton School in Philadelphia.

had a job at his father's company, Donald knew it was important to learn as much as he could. After two years, Donald changed schools and went to the Wharton School at the University of Pennsylvania. He studied **economics** instead of film, but that wasn't the end of his movie star dreams.

Chapter 3
Big Business, Big Screen!

Donald worked hard at his father's company. He had lots of ideas about how to make it better. In 1971, he became the head of the company. It was a bumpy start. In 1973, the government said he had **discriminated** against African Americans by not renting houses to them. Donald agreed to make sure anyone who wanted to live in his buildings would be allowed to.

Donald had a lot of success in real estate. He bought buildings and made lots of money. In 1979 he bought the property that would become Trump Tower. It is on the same block where he had marched in the Columbus Day parade when he was young.

Trump Tower is one of the most famous buildings in New York. Donald's buildings are easy to recognize because he likes to put his name on them in gold letters.

Donald stands by pictures of his company's buildings in 1980.

13

THE TRUMP FAMILY

Donald didn't settle for having a big business. He has a big family as well! With his first wife, Ivana Zelníčková, he had three children: Donald Jr., Ivanka, and Eric. The marriage ended in 1992. He married his second wife, actress Marla Maples, after the birth of their daughter, Tiffany. Donald and Marla divorced in 1999. In 2005 he married Slovenian model Melania Knauss. Their son, Barron, was born in 2006, the same year Melania became a citizen.

Trump Tower is fifty-eight stories tall.

Donald poses with two of his children, Eric and Ivanka, at Yankee Stadium.

TRUMP GOES HOLLYWOOD

Donald became famous around the country thanks to his big personality and his work in New York real estate. This allowed him to reach his dream of working in Hollywood by playing himself in several movies.

Donald has had small roles in twenty different movies and TV shows.

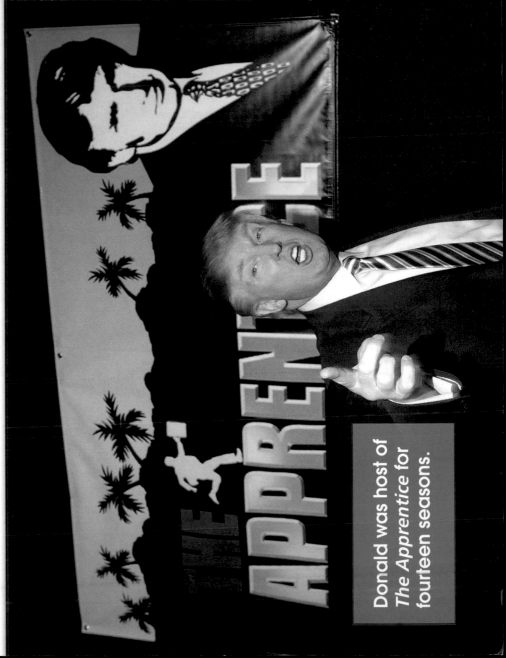

Donald was host of *The Apprentice* for fourteen seasons.

When Donald was not playing a funny version of himself he was often cast to play a businessman. Donald loved having small parts in movies and television shows, but he wanted to do something bigger.

In 2004 Donald became a host on his **reality television** show *The Apprentice*. On the show, **contestants** would compete at tasks that Donald created to test their business skills.

At the end of every episode, Donald chose one contestant to leave the show by saying "You're fired!" The final winner was offered a job in one of Donald's companies.

Donald appeared on the show until 2015, when he made his biggest move yet.

Donald Says:
"One thing about television, it brings out personality."

CHAPTER 4
THE WINNING CANDIDATE

In 2015, Donald decided to try something new. He said that he was running for president of the United States. He had a long history of giving his opinions on political subjects, but he had never run for office.

Donald ran as a member of the Republican Party. In United States politics, the two main parties are the Democrats and the Republicans. Winning the Republican nomination was not easy. There were sixteen other people running against him. While many people liked that Donald always said what was on his mind, others found the things he said to be rude or mean. Sometimes he said things that many commentators and other politicians believed were untrue.

The primary election decides who will represent each party in the general (main) election. After a tough race, Donald won the Republican primary. He broke the record

Donald Says:

"I promise you that I will not let you down. We will do a great job."

for most primary votes in the history of the Republican Party. He received nearly fourteen million votes.

THE LONG CAMPAIGN

After the primary election, Donald ran against the Democratic nominee, Hillary Rodham Clinton. As the former First Lady, a senator, and **secretary of state**, Hillary was a tough opponent to beat. But many people thought Donald would bring something new to the role of president because he had never been in politics. One thing everyone agreed on was that Donald was like no other candidate they had ever seen before.

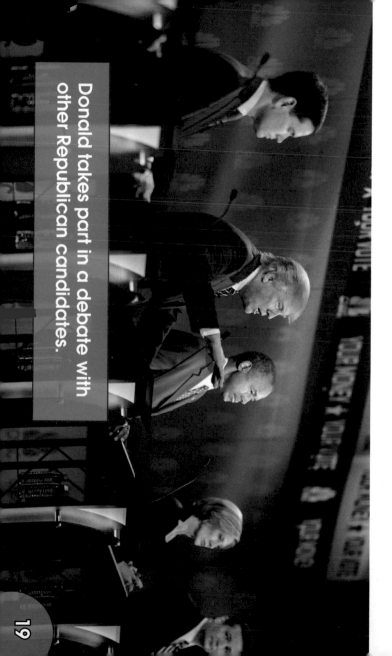

Donald takes part in a debate with other Republican candidates.

Trump greets his supporters during the campaign.

After a very close race, Donald won in the **Electoral College.** The election was so close, in fact, that Hillary actually received more popular votes than Donald. But Donald would be the next president of the United States. Some people marched to show Donald that they didn't agree with his ideas. Donald spoke to the country and promised he would be a good president for everyone.

Donald is the fifth American president to win the Electoral College but not the popular vote.

people were glad that Donald had won, but in some cities,

After winning the election, Donald Trump promised to be "president to all Americans."

TIMELINE

1946 Donald John Trump is born in Queens, New York, on June 14.

1959 Begins studies at New York Military Academy.

1964 Attends Fordham University in New York.

1966 Transfers to University of Pennsylvania.

1968 Graduates with a bachelor of science degree in finance.

1971 Is given control of his father's business, which he renames the Trump Organization.

1977 Marries Ivana Zelníčková; son Donald Jr. is born later that year.

1981 Daughter Ivanka is born.

1983 Completes building Trump Tower on Fifth Avenue in Manhattan.

1984 Completes building his casino Harrah's at Trump Plaza in Atlantic City, New Jersey; son Eric is born.

1992 Divorces Ivana.

1993 Daughter, Tiffany, is born; marries Marla Maples three months later.

1999 Divorces Marla.

2003 Becomes host of *The Apprentice.*

2005 Marries Melania Knauss.

2006 Son Barron is born.

2015 Wins the Republican Primary nomination.

2016 Wins election for president of the United States.

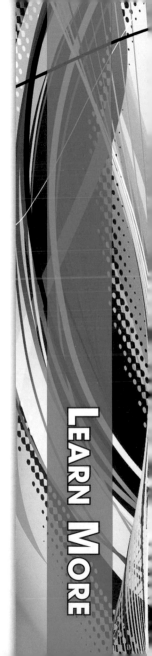

LEARN MORE

Books

Baicker, Karen. *The Election Activity Book.* New York, NY: Scholastic, 2012.

Ringstad, Arnold. *Weird-But-True Facts About U.S. Presidents.* Mankato, MN: Child's World, 2013.

Shea, Therese. *How a Skyscraper Is Built.* New York, NY: Gareth Stevens, 2016.

Websites

Official Trump Campaign
www.donaldjtrump.com
Learn all about the 2016 presidential campaign.

Trump Tower
www.trumptowerny.com
Read all about Trump's famous building.

INDEX

Published in 2018 by Enslow Publishing, LLC
101 W. 23rd Street, Suite 240 New York, NY 10011

Copyright © 2018 by Enslow Publishing, LLC
All rights reserved.

No part of this book make be reproduced by any means without the written permission of the publisher.

Library of Congress Cataloguing-in-Publication Data
Names: Santos, Rita, author.
Title: Donald Trump : businessman and president / Rita Santos.
Description: New York, NY : Enslow Publishing, LLC., 2018. | Series title: Junior biographies | Includes bibliographical references and index. |
Audience: Grade 3 to 5.
Identifiers: ISBN 9780766086661 (library bound) | ISBN 9780766087873 (paperback) | ISBN 9780766087880 (6-pack)
Subjects: Trump, Donald, 1946–Juvenile literature. | Businessmen–United States–Biography–Juvenile literature. | Real estate developers–United States–Biography–Juvenile literature. | Celebrities–United States–Biography–Juvenile literature. | Television personalities–United States–Biography–Juvenile literature. | Presidential candidates–United States–Biography–Juvenile literature.
Classification: DDC 333.33092 B

Printed in the United States of America

To Our Readers: We have done our best to make sure all websites in this book were active and appropriate when we went to press. However, the author and the publisher have no control over and assume no liability for the material available on those websites or on any websites they may link to. Any comments or suggestions can be sent by e-mail to customerservice@enslow.com.

Photo Credits: Cover, p. 1 Tinseltown/Shutterstock. com; p. 4 Mike Pont/WireImage/Getty Images; p. 6 Ted Pink/Alamy Stock Photo; p. 7 H. Armstrong Roberts/ ClassicStock/Getty Images; p. 8 © AP Images; p. 10 John Greim/LightRocket/Getty Images; p. 13 Ted Horowitz/ Corbis Documentary/Getty Images; p. 14 Alan Schein Photography/Corbis Documentary/Getty Images; p. 15 Robin Platzer/The LIFE Images Collection/Getty Images; p. 16 ZUMA Press, Inc./Alamy Stock Photo; p. 19 Bloomberg/Getty Images; p. 20 Julie Dermansky/ Corbis News/Getty Images; p. 21 Mark Wilson/Getty Images; back cover, pp. 2, 3, 22, 23 (curves graphic) Alena Kazlouskaya/Shutterstock.com; interior pages (stars and stripes) skdesigns/DigitalVision Vectors/ Getty Images.